ABUNDANT TRUTH INTERNATIONAL MINISTRIES

Ministry Guides Series

The Believer's Guide to the Teaching Ministry

A Comprehensive Study of the Teaching Ministry in the Church

Roderick Levi Evans

The Believer's Guide to the Teaching Ministry

A Comprehensive Study of the Teaching Ministry in the Church

All Rights Reserved ©2024 by Roderick L. Evans

No part of this book may be reproduced or transmitted in any form or by any means, graphic, electronic, or mechanical, including photocopying, recording, taping, or by any information storage or retrieval system, without the permission in writing from the publisher.

Front & Back Cover Designs by Abundant Truth Publishing
Cover designed by Freepik

Abundant Truth Publishing
an imprint of Abundant Truth International Ministries
For information address:
Abundant Truth International
P.O. Box 126
Camden, NC 27921

Unless otherwise indicated, all of the scripture quotations are taken from the *Authorized King James Version* of the Bible. Scripture quotations marked with NIV are taken from the *New International Version* of the Bible. Scripture quotations marked with NASV are taken from the *New American Standard Version* of the Bible. Scripture quotations marked with Amplified are taken from the *Amplified Bible*.

ISBN: 978-1-60141-639-1

Printed in the United States of America

Contents

Introduction
Book 1 - The Building of the Teacher: 1
The Preparation of the Teacher and the
Teaching Disciple for Ministry and Service
Introduction   3

Chapter 1- The Vision of the Teacher   7
The Role of Faith   11
The Role of Hardships   12

Chapter 2 - Hallmark of the Teacher   15
Surrender   17
Submit   19
Sell-out Completely   21

Chapter 3 - Building of the Teacher   23
Spirit of the Lord   26
Spirit of Wisdom and Understanding   27
Spirit of Counsel and Might   29
Spirit of Knowledge and Fear   30

Chapter 4 - The Teacher's Character   33
Love   36
Joy   38

Contents (cont.)

Peace	40
Patience	41
Kindness	42
Faithfulness	44
Gentleness	45
Self-Control	46

Book 2 - Now Concerning Teachers: **49**
Establishing the Role of the Teacher in the Body of Christ

Preface	51
Introduction	53

Chapter 1 – What is a Teacher?	**57**
The Tasks of the Teaching Ministry	61
The Tenant of the Teaching Ministry	64

Chapter 2 – The Call of a Teacher	**67**
New to the Call to Teach	70
Noticing the Call to Teach	75
Navigating the Call to Teach	83

Contents (cont.)

Chapter 3 – The Office of the Teacher	**91**
Nine Functions of the Teaching Office	93
Focus of Teachers	105
Chapter 4 – The Roles of the Teacher	**107**
Teachers as Instructors	110
Teachers as Trainers	113
Teaching Disciples	118
Chapter 5 – False Teachers	**121**
Characteristics of False Ministers	126
Characteristics of False Teachers	133
Book 3 – The Training of the Teaching Disciple: The Preparation of the Teaching Disciple for Ministry and Service	**141**
Introduction	143
Prologue - Understanding Anointings	149
Anointings in the Old Testament	152
Anointings in the New Testament	157
Office versus Anointing	164

Contents (cont.)

Chapter 1 - Teaching Disciples as Instructors	**169**
Skilled in Function	171
Skilled in Information	172
Skilled in Instruction	173
Chapter 2 - Teaching Disciples as Tutors	**175**
Teach from Experience	177
Teach from Versatility	178
Teach through Application	180
Chapter 3 - Character Traits of Teaching Disciples	**183**
Humility of the Teaching Disciple	186
Hallmarks of the Teaching Disciple	187
Chapter 4 – Identifying the Teaching Anointing	**191**
Teachers of the Word	193
Teachers of Application	194
Teachers of Action	195
Teachers of Interpretation	197

Contents (cont.)

Chapter 5 – Walking in the Teaching Anointing   **201**
Consistent Study   203
Persistent Prayer   204
Insistent Submission   205

Bibliography   **209**

Introduction

Ministry and service are gifts from God. The ministries are multifaceted and sometimes complex. The Ministry Guides Series is designed to offer information that will strengthen, enlighten, and encourage those involved in Christian ministry.

In this publication

In this book, we will bring clarity to the roles of teachers, the functionality of the teaching ministry, and the expressions of the teaching gift. This study is comprised of 3 distinct works on the teaching office and gift:

1) The Building of the Teacher: The Preparation of the Teacher and the Teaching Disciple for Ministry and Service

2) Now Concerning Teachers: Establishing the Role of the Teacher in the Body of Christ

3) The Training of the Teaching Disciple: The Preparation of the Teaching Disciple for Ministry and Service

It is our prayer that a greater understanding and appreciation for the teaching gift and ministry will be achieved.

THE BELIEVER'S GUIDE TO THE TEACHING MINISTRY — A Comprehensive Study of the Teaching Ministry in the Church

-Book 1-

The Building of the Teacher:

The Preparation of the Teacher and the Teaching Disciple for Ministry and Service

Ministry Guides Series

THE BELIEVER'S GUIDE TO THE TEACHING MINISTRY — A Comprehensive Study of the Teaching Ministry in the Church

The training of a teacher is oftentimes unending. God will allow disruption in every area of his life. It will prepare him for service. Those called to the teaching office should understand that preparation for ministry is in the development of godly character, characterized by love. If this is done, the teacher will never fail as he discharges his ministry. In this book, we will discuss how God builds the teacher for ministry.

THE BELIEVER'S GUIDE TO THE TEACHING MINISTRY — A Comprehensive Study of the Teaching Ministry in the Church

Introduction

Ministry and service in the kingdom of God is a privilege. God calls every member of the Body of Christ to serve for the benefit and welfare of the Body of Christ. However, we must remember that there are personal preparations that God requires for service.

The Potter's Wheel Study Series is designed to help believers recognize and apply the personal preparation that God implements for those called to minister and to serve. It is our prayer that the minister and the laymen will respond to God's personal preparations for ministry and service.

In this Publication

The teacher's ministry comes with a charge to equip, instruct, and mature the Body of Christ. These are only parts of the teacher's ministry. His ministry serves as a reflection of Christ, the living Word.

Therefore, the teacher's character has to be solid. God will take teachers through tests, trials, and temptations in order to prepare them for ministry. It is the only way they will be able to teach "line upon line" and "precept upon precept."

The training of a teacher is oftentimes unending. God will allow disruption in every area of his life. It will prepare him for service.

Those called to the teaching office should understand that preparation for ministry is in the development of godly character, characterized by love. If this is done, the teacher will never fail as he discharges his ministry. In this book, we will discuss how God builds the teacher for ministry.

THE BELIEVER'S GUIDE TO THE TEACHING MINISTRY — A Comprehensive Study of the Teaching Ministry in the Church

-Chapter 1-

The Vision of the Teacher

Jeremiah's Vision

Jeremiah prophesied to Judah during a time of great rebellion and sin against God. At the beginning of his commission, Jeremiah received visions from the Lord.

> *Moreover the word of the LORD came unto me, saying, Jeremiah, what seest thou? And I said, I see a rod of an almond tree. Then said the LORD unto me, Thou hast well seen: for I will hasten my word to perform it. And the word of the LORD came unto me the second time, saying, What seest thou? And I said, I see a*

seething pot; and the face thereof is toward the north. Then the LORD said unto me, Out of the north an evil shall break forth upon all the inhabitants of the land. Jer 1:11-14 (KJV)

When we consider this, we discover that God shows Jeremiah two things. The first is a rod of an almond tree. It meant God's word would come forth.

The teacher has to be convinced of the validity and authenticity of the word of God. Every promise and exhortation of scripture is law to the teacher.

The Role of Faith

God will impart an unwavering faith and trust in the scriptures in those called to teach. They will be able to teach with all authority and grace. The rod of an almond tree also represents the teacher's resolve to grow personally while causing other to grow in the faith.

Without this unwavering faith, the teacher will not be able to stand against criticism and opposition to the truths of the Bible. Unwavering faith in the scriptures is the foundational building block to a teacher's spiritual make up.

The second thing that Jeremiah saw was a seething pot. It was a boiling pot of water. We know that this represented God's judgment coming upon the nation.

However, in the life of the teacher, the boiling pot represents the many trials, tests, and tribulations that the teacher will experience.

The Role of Hardships

God will pour out hardships to humble the teacher, create compassion in the teacher, and mature the teacher. Teachers will endure many hardships before and during the course of their ministries. God allows the teacher to experience the hot waters of life that they may know the power of the word.

Experiences come so that they will be able to teach others, not only in word, but also by personal application of the scriptures. John stated that Christ was the 'word made flesh.'

The word comes alive to the teacher as he is challenged to apply it to his daily life. The hardships come so that the teacher will be a doer of what he teaches. The teacher becomes an extension of the 'word made flesh' as he faces obstacles and overcomes through the daily application of the Word.

-Chapter 2-

Hallmark of the Teacher:

Self-Denial

A teacher who is not disciplined will damage the Church. To protect the teacher and the Church, God takes teachers through transitions that will bring them to a place of self-death and denial.

There are three things that an individual has to do in order to die to self. These three things have to be implemented by the teacher for success in ministry.

Surrender

The first step teacher has to do is surrender to the will of God. The will of God is not only in a teaching, but also in becoming like Christ.

> *For whom he did foreknow, he also did predestinate to be conformed to the image of his Son, that he might be the firstborn among many brethren. (Romans 8:29)*

Teachers have to know that the will of God for their ministries begins with becoming like Christ. The teacher's ministry has to become secondary to character development. The teacher who surrenders to this will be a pillar in the faith.

Submit

Teachers have to be in subjection to the authority of the Word of God. Submitting to the Word not only entails teaching it, but consistent application of the Word in daily living.

In order to do this, teachers have to believe that the scriptures, as recorded, are the final authority on righteousness, religion, and relationship with God. Paul states,

> *All scripture is given by inspiration of God, and is profitable for doctrine, for reproof, for correction, for*

instruction in righteousness: That the man of God may be perfect, thoroughly furnished unto all good works. (II Timothy 3:16-17)

The teachers submit to the authority of the Word by having unwavering belief in it. It will challenge the heart and mind of the teacher to walk in righteousness.

The Word exposes the inner thoughts and intents of the heart of the teacher. Without it, the teacher may deceive himself and not be able to discharge fully the ministry properly.

Sell-out Completely

Finally, teachers have to sell-out completely to the Lord. When we usually hear the term "sell-out," it is usually in a derogatory manner. Someone who is a sell-out has forsaken an alliance for another. This is what the teacher we must do for effective service.

The teacher has to forsake the world and the lusts thereof. If the teacher is not careful, the world will ensnare him, the alliances of men will entrap him, and personal desires will envelop him.

Selling out to the Lord guards the

teacher against selfish motives and means in ministry. The teacher has to forsake selfish motives, ambitions, and desires. These attributes will bring stagnation to the ministry. The teacher has to live by the hallmark of self-denial. It is what holds God's building process together.

-Chapter 3-

Building of the Teacher:

The Stem of Jesse

God develops selflessness and love in the teacher to build them into faithful servants.

There are general characteristics that every teacher possesses because of Christ's building process. Since the teacher has to instruct others concerning Christ.

God will build them to reflect Christ by forming the attributes of Christ in them. Isaiah's description of the Stem of Jesse gives a clear depiction of how God builds the teacher.

And there shall come forth a rod out of the stem of Jesse, and a Branch shall grow out of his roots: And the spirit of the LORD shall rest upon him, the spirit of wisdom and understanding, the spirit of counsel and might, the spirit of knowledge and of the fear of the LORD; And shall make him of quick understanding in the fear of the LORD. Isaiah 11:1-3 (KJV)

Spirit of the Lord

The first block of the teacher's build is the presence of the Holy Spirit. The teacher has to know that ministry should be based upon revelation and inspiration, not upon intellect and opinion.

> *Which things also we speak, not in the words which man's wisdom teacheth, but which the Holy Ghost teacheth; comparing spiritual things with spiritual. 1 Cor 2:13 (KJV)*

The teacher has to depend on the greatest teacher in order to teach effectively in the Church. He needs to know the voice of the Holy Spirit.

Spirit of Wisdom and Understanding

The second block is wisdom and understanding. The teacher cannot teach according to the wisdom and precepts of men. His doctrine has to reflect the eternal truths of God.

Howbeit we speak wisdom among them that are perfect: yet not the wisdom of this world, nor of the princes of this world, that come to nought: But we speak the wisdom of God in a mystery, even the hidden wisdom, which God ordained before the world unto our glory. 1 Cor 2:6-7 (KJV)

The teacher has to endeavor to teach doctrine that will clearly affirm God's existence, Christ's salvation, and the

Christian faith. The teacher has to understand the truths of the Kingdom of God and be able to bring others into this understanding.

Spirit of Counsel and Might

The third block is counsel and might. The teacher has to know how to show others how to apply the principles of the scriptures. The spirit of counsel is needed to do this effectively.

In addition, the teacher has to be strong and mighty in the scriptures, having a solid understanding. Remember what was said of Apollos.

And a certain Jew named Apollos, born at Alexandria, an eloquent man, and mighty in the scriptures, came to Ephesus. Acts 18:24 (KJV)

Spirit of Knowledge and Fear

It is understood that the teacher will have a profound knowledge of God and His Word. However, knowledge has to be coupled with fear (or reverence) for God. Reverence for God will keep the teacher from promoting himself and erroneous doctrines.

The characteristics of Christ form the building blocks to the teacher. If the teacher has these in place, the ministry will be effective and solid resulting in mature disciples of Christ in the Church.

-Chapter 4-

The Teacher's Character

Teachers bring men to a knowledge of what is written. This task sometimes causes teachers to become vulnerable to legalism and pride. In order for the teaching ministry in them to remain vibrant and life-giving, teachers have to balance their knowledge of the letter with the revelation of the Holy Spirit. Teachers need the fruit of the Spirit to govern their characters as they minister in the Church.

The teacher's character finds it definition within the personality of the Spirit. To temper their knowledge of the scriptures, the teacher has to develop the fruit of the Spirit. It is the standard for their characters.

Their character has to mirror the fruit of the Spirit. The fruit of the Spirit must then become the "fruit of the teacher's character."

Love

Love has to be the foundation of the teacher's ministry. Paul revealed that gifts in operation without love are ineffective. Since teachers promote doctrines and principles, some can become impersonal in the delivery and presentation of the messages given.

Their knowledge of the scriptures should bring men into a greater understanding of the love of God.

Charity suffereth long, and is kind; charity envieth not; charity vaunteth not itself, is not puffed up, doth not behave itself unseemly, seeketh not her own, is not easily provoked, thinketh no evil; rejoiceth not in iniquity, but rejoiceth in the truth; Beareth all things, believeth all things, hopeth all things, endureth all things. (I Corinthians 13:4-7)

The teacher has to have a love for

God and the people to whom they minister. If they do not, they may teach the right principles, but apply them improperly as they minister.

They have to administer the principles and doctrines of Christ with His heart and mind. The teacher's demonstration of love must match Paul's description of love as recorded in I Corinthians 13.

Joy

Teachers are carriers of the doctrines and mysteries of Christ. Though they are serious about the Word and its delivery, they should also be people of joy.

While writing to the Romans, Paul dealt with strife between believers over non-doctrinal issues. At the end of his discourse, he said these words,

> *For the kingdom of God is not eating and drinking, but righteousness, JOY, and peace in the Holy Spirit. (Romans 14:17 NASV Emphasis mine)*

Teachers can become so consumed with promoting right doctrine, they can forget that the scriptures reveal that there is joy in service to God. They must teach believers how to walk in the joy that comes with membership in the kingdom of God.

Peace

Teachers must be ministers of peace. Their quest for doctrinal stability puts them in the middle of conflict. However, they are not to allow their pursuit for right doctrine to cause personal feelings to rise in ministry.

Teachers have to be led by peace and inspire peace in their audiences. Jesus prayed that we would have peace, though the gospel sets us against the world.

Peace I leave with you, my peace I give unto you: not as the world giveth, give I unto you. Let not your heart be troubled, neither let it be afraid. (John 14:27)

Some teachers are always cynical and frustrated with the Church because of the presence of false doctrines. However, they have to reflect peace as they strive to bring balance and insight into the Church.

Patience

Patience is one of the necessary character traits of teachers. Some teachers forget that God gives their understanding to them. They have to exercise patience as others strive to understand and apply what is taught. Teachers need patience as they minister to the Church.

Teachers are not to become the Church critics. Some feel their role is to correct, correct, and correct! They have to understand that their insight of the Word is given to promote stability and unity. They are not to become judges of the Church and other ministries.

Kindness

Teachers have to be kind. Because they exercise great understanding in spiritual truths, some feel superior to others. They may treat others as if they are subordinates because they lack the anointing and understanding that they possess.

Some teachers justify impoliteness by stating that others just are not on their level.

...not self-willed, not soon angry, not given to wine, no striker, not given to filthy lucre; But a lover of hospitality, a lover of good men, sober, just, holy, temperate. (Titus 1:7-8)

Teachers have to know how to

conduct themselves as recipients of the revelation and grace of God. With this understanding, their lives at home and among the saints must be in demonstration of the kindness of God.

Faithfulness

Every teacher must be faithful to the call of God. He must demonstrate loyalty to Christ, the Church, and the Word. Teachers have to be unwavering in their commitment to God in the presentation of their ministries.

Let a man so account of us, as of the ministers of Christ, and stewards of the mysteries of God. Moreover it is required in stewards, that a man be found faithful. (I Corinthians 4:1-2)

Since the teaching ministry can bring hardship to true teachers, faithfulness will sustain them in times of opposition. One of God's attributes is faithfulness; therefore, the teacher has to be faithful as he carries out the will of God.

Gentleness

Teachers have to be gentle as they minister to the saints. They may have the right words, but the wrong delivery. In addition, they are to be gentle with family and friends. It is a required trait of the servant of the Lord.

And the servant of the Lord must not strive; but be gentle unto all men, apt to teach, patient, In meekness instructing those that oppose themselves; if God peradventure will give them repentance of the truth (II Timothy 2:24)

Self-Control

Teachers are to exercise self-control in every affair of their lives. Self-control is needed in the pulpit, on the mission field, or in their homes.

Not given to wine, no striker, not greedy of filthy lucre; but patient, not a brawler, not covetous; one that ruleth well his own house, having his children in subjection with all gravity. (I Timothy 3:3-4)

Some teachers feel that they always have to speak up and correct everyone. Anyone called to the teaching ministry must remember that success in ministry is not in being right, but in the maintenance of character, integrity, and conduct as they minister. Godly character will determine the level of success of the teachers as they fulfill their functions in the Church.

For a full examination of the teaching ministry, please see my book, **"Now Concerning Teachers: Establishing the Role of the Teacher in the Body of Christ."**

THE BELIEVER'S GUIDE TO THE TEACHING MINISTRY — A Comprehensive Study of the Teaching Ministry in the Church

-Book 2-

Now Concerning Teachers:

Establishing the Role of the Teacher in the Body of Christ

This book was written to bring clarity and understanding to the teaching office and the teaching anointing. This information will help individuals to recognize the operations of this anointing in their lives and in the lives of others. It is our hope that believers will develop a greater respect and appreciation for the teaching office and gift.

Preface

The teaching ministry is important to the furtherance of the Kingdom of God and the Church. It is my prayer that the information presented in this work will bring clarity, appreciation, and understanding to the teaching ministry.

Numerous works have been produced which highlight the ministries listed in Ephesians 4. This book is to be used in connection with other publications. Many authors focus on the functions of the teacher and minister. My intent is to bring balance by focusing on the character requirements of those walking in this office and possessing this anointing.

Roderick Levi Evans

THE BELIEVER'S GUIDE TO THE TEACHING MINISTRY — A Comprehensive Study of the Teaching Ministry in the Church

Introduction

At His departure, Jesus instructed the disciples to go to Jerusalem to await the promise of the Father. On the day of Pentecost, this promise was fulfilled with the outpouring of the Holy Spirit.

The Holy Spirit was given so that the work of Jesus Christ would continue on the earth. The Ministerial Endowments Series is designed to bring clarity to the gifts and ministries given to the Church. It is our prayer that believers will be enlightened and encouraged.

THE BELIEVER'S GUIDE TO THE TEACHING MINISTRY — A Comprehensive Study of the Teaching Ministry in the Church

In the publication:

The scriptures reveal that God has set ministries and gifts in the Church. The ministries of the apostle and the prophet provided the foundation for the Church. However, their ministries alone could not advance the Church. Thus, God set other ministries within the Church; more specifically, the teaching ministry. This ministry is important for the equipping, perfecting, and maturing of the saints.

In the pages of this book, we will discuss the ministry of the teacher in detail. A proper understanding of this ministry will help individuals recognize and appreciate its functionality in the Church.

-Chapter 1-

What is a Teacher?

And God hath set some in the church, thirdly teachers... (I Cor. 12:28)

Teachers are anointed to expound upon the word of God. Often times, they are anointed apologists of the Word. They will look at the Word: line upon line and precept upon precept. They possess the revelation and knowledge of God concerning the scriptures. Their ministry is devalued at times, but their ministry is very important. Let us look at this ministry more closely.

The word teacher originates from the Greek word, didaskalos, which means an instructor. Some commentators have determined that Ephesians 4:11 should be read pastor-teacher instead of pastors and teachers.

They assert that it is not one of the ministry offices. However, after God set apostles and prophets in the Church, He then placed teachers. This is so the Church can be grounded in Him.

Teachers are chosen to reveal the principles and doctrines of the faith. They are anointed to communicate biblical truths in a practical manner. Before going into detail concerning the ministry of the teacher, we want to present some foundational truths concerning their ministries.

The Tasks of the Teaching Ministry

Teachers help the Church to grow through their ministry. Teachers provide systematic guidelines for living in the Kingdom. Apollos was a recognized teacher in the early church. The Corinthian church respected him as a teacher.

I have planted, Apollos watered; but God gave the increase. (I Corinthians 3:6) see also Acts 18:24 -28.

The office of the teacher is a valid ministry in the Church. Some commentators have determined that

Ephesians 4:11 should be read pastor-teacher instead of pastors and teachers. Therefore, it is not one of the ministry offices.

However, after God set apostles and prophets in the Church, He then placed teachers. This is so the Church can be grounded in Him. We should not receive this ministry as boring or useless, it is vital to the foundation of the Church.

And God hath set some in the Church, first apostles, and secondarily prophets, thirdly teachers... (I Corinthians 12:28a)

Now there were in the Church at Antioch certain prophets and teachers... (Acts 13:1a)

Signs and wonders should follow their ministry as well as the other offices. Those who are called to this office should expect God to move in their ministries. God always confirms His word.

The same came to Jesus by night, and said unto him, Rabbi, we know that thou art a teacher come from God: for no man can do these miracles that thou doest, except God be with him.(John 3:2)

The teacher's primary ministry is to expound upon the Word. The Word is most effective when it is taught and demonstrated (signs and wonders following).

The Tenant of the Teaching Ministry

Teachers abide by one major tenant or rule. They want to see the people of God informed.

They will work to see that the believers have the right information that will lead them to God. Teachers are concerned for the growth and stability of the Church.

They have the responsibility to promote spiritual truth and insights through proper explanation and application of the scriptures. They will have insight into what God is saying in the scriptures. However, they must be careful not to misinterpret God's personal involvement in an individual's life by the misappropriation of scriptures.

Teachers must be careful not to become so dogmatic that they do not allow the Spirit of God to speak through them. They must guard themselves against spiritual pride because of the knowledge they possess. They may begin to teach against something that is of God because of personal opinion. The tenant that they abide by causes vulnerability in this area.

-Chapter 2-

The Call of a Teacher

God calls individuals to the teaching office in many ways. In the Old and New Testaments, we discover that God called men in different manners. God's call to the teaching office is important. The teacher's ministry is needed if the Church is going to grow in grace and knowledge of Jesus Christ. Therefore, God has to establish the one called to this ministry through how He calls them.

There are individuals who occupy want to be teachers without any anointing or grace to do it. Education does not qualify one to teach in the Church. A clear undeniable call and endowment from the Lord is necessary. Always remember that a person who may teach by profession is not always the one who is anointed to teach in the Church. It is a God-given ministry.

This chapter is designed to help believers recognize the call to teach upon others and themselves. We will look at scriptural examples of how the Lord called individuals to understand the call of the teacher.

New to the Call to Teach

The call of a teacher is unique from

others in one respect. Though all ministers receive their calling from the Lord, the call to teach comes with a direct challenge to instruct and educate the Body of Christ.

We have previously stated that one who teaches by profession is not the qualifying factor for a teacher in the Church. God calls teachers in order to ground the people in spiritual truth and understanding. Consequently, those who are called to teach need to be sure of their call.

Since the New Testament introduces us to the ministry of the teacher, which developed thirdly in the Church, we will use two main examples from these texts to understand the teacher's call.

Jesus & Paul

Paul was an apostle of the Lord, without question. However, we know by the scriptures that Paul also occupied the office of the teacher. Repeatedly, in his texts, he reaffirmed the call to teach.

Whereunto I am ordained a preacher, and an apostle, (I speak the truth in Christ, and lie not;) a teacher of the Gentiles in faith and verity. 1 Tim 2:7 (KJV)

Whereunto I am appointed a preacher, and an apostle, and a teacher of the Gentiles. 2 Tim 1:11 (KJV)

Paul realized that in his apostleship, there was a definite call to teach. If you want to teach, make sure you have a definite call from the Lord. Without such, you could be operating in an area that you should not. All believers are to know and understand biblical truths, but God anoints individuals to teach.

Paul assurance of his call to teach came from his experience with Jesus. After his conversion, Jesus took him aside and taught him the gospel. This reveals that if you are called to teach, you will experience impartations of knowledge and understanding from the Lord.

For I have received of the Lord that which also I delivered unto you...1 Cor 11:23 (KJV)

Not all of your doctrine will be from men, but Christ will personally reveal truths to you. All of these things take place when you are new to the call and continue throughout the life and ministry of the teacher.

Noticing the Call to Teach

Once an individual notices and receives a call to the teaching office, there must be a response and answer to the Lord. Before the teacher is processed for service (discussed in the next chapter), there are certain things that the future teacher has to do.

Study the Word

The teacher's office comes with great commission – instruct members of the Body of Christ. He will be responsible for spiritual growth, development, and advancement of those in the Church.

Therefore, the teacher has to have a clear understanding of the word of God. He has to know how to make the word of God applicable to lives of the people. A sure of way of this is consistently study the word of God.

> *Study to shew thyself approved unto God, a workman that needeth not to be ashamed, rightly dividing the word of truth. 2 Tim 2:15 (KJV)*

You cannot teach what you do not know. The teacher has to live by Paul's exhortation to Timothy. The teacher who will be effectively will consistently be in pursuit for the knowledge of God and His word.

Knowledge of the scriptures makes one wise concerning salvation. The one who is called to teach will need wisdom in connection with their knowledge. This is done through the study and dissection of the scriptures.

And that from a child thou hast known the holy scriptures, which are able to make thee wise unto salvation through faith which is in Christ Jesus. 2 Tim 3:15 (KJV)

Study Others

After perceiving a call to the teaching office, a time of learning is needed to ensure the teacher's success. The teacher is called in a personal way, but God will use others to perfect the teaching ministry in an individual. Earlier, we spoke of Paul's call to teach.

Paul's experience reveals the personal way in which Jesus calls and equips a teacher. However, the story of Apollos reveals that God will use others to aid in one's acceptance of the office to teach. In the Book of Acts introduces us to

Apollos. The scriptures say that he was mighty in the Old Testament scriptures.

And a certain Jew named Apollos, born at Alexandria, an eloquent man, and mighty in the scriptures, came to Ephesus. This man was instructed in the way of the Lord; and being fervent in the spirit, he spake and taught diligently the things of the Lord, knowing only the baptism of John. Acts 18:24-25 (KJV)

Apollos knew the way of the Lord. This means that he believed in the God of Israel. He understood spiritual truths, but his knowledge was not complete. He was not ready to be loosed upon the Church as a teacher. God allowed others in the faith to instruct him which proved beneficial to his ministry in the Church.

> *And he began to speak boldly in the synagogue: whom when Aquila and Priscilla had heard, they took him unto them, and*
>
> *expounded unto him the way of God more perfectly. Acts 18:26 (KJV)*

If you are called to teach, the input of others will be beneficial. Apollos humbled himself and received from others. The one called to teach has to know that he needs others though Christ will give him understanding also.

Study Yourself

A call to the teaching office places one in a position of authority. Teachers, consequently, have to have safeguards in place against spiritual pride and deception.

Examine yourselves, whether ye be in the faith; prove your own selves.
2 Cor 13:5 (KJV)

Paul challenged the Corinthians to examine themselves. The one called to teach must be humble and teachable. They have to be aware of their personal weaknesses.

Continual self-examination will help them to remain faithful to Christ, committed to the advancement of members of the Body, and settled in the personal walks with Jesus.

Therefore, my beloved brethren, be ye stedfast, unmoveable, always abounding in the work of the Lord, forasmuch as ye know that your labour is not in vain in the Lord.
1 Cor 15:58 (KJV)

Navigating the Call to Teach

Since the teaching office is a foundational ministry, bringing men into the stature of the fullness of Christ, those who want to operate in this ministry must be certain and clear in recognizing and accepting the call to teach in their lives and in the lives of others.

Therefore, in concluding our examination of the call of a teacher, we will discuss briefly certain signs of the call to teach. This will help in the acceptance of the call to teach on an individual's life.

Love of Christ

The individual who is called to the teaching office will have a profound love for God and Christ. He will speak of Christ in the most personal terms. He will also have a love and deeply personal concern for others in the Body of Christ.

The love of Christ will bring balance to the knowledge that the teacher will receive. It causes the teacher to expound upon the written word with a personal zeal and reverence.

We must remember, however, that all believers are to love Christ and the Church. God will impart a deep compassion to those called so that they will passionately defend and promote spiritual growth. Though the teacher will have this level of love and compassion, any believer is a candidate for it. Again, this is given as a sign of a call to the teaching office.

Love of the Scriptures

Teachers will have a deep love and reverence for the scriptures. Those called will love to get into conversations about the Bible. They will spend long hours studying and meditating upon the word of God. They will possess an insatiable hunger for spiritual truth.

Problematic scriptures will trouble them until they find a solution. They will want to know so that they will be able to help others in the Body of Christ. God will do this to the one called so that they will be equipped to teach others.

All scripture is given by inspiration of God, and is profitable for doctrine, for reproof, for correction, for instruction in righteousness: That the man of God may be perfect, thoroughly furnished unto all good works. 2 Tim 3:16-17 (KJV)

Those called to teach will not find bible study, boring or preaching, ineffective. They will learn from all aspects of the presentation of the word of God. It will supplement their personal study and pursuit of knowledge and understanding in the Church.

Love of the Body

Teachers, again, will have a deep love for Christ and the Church. Because of this, those who are called to this office will be committed to prayer. Much of their prayer will be for the Church, its members, and for a deeper understanding of the Word. They have a desire to see Christ formed in those whom they teach. Therefore, consistent prayer for themselves and others will characterize the teacher's personal life.

In his letters, the apostle Paul would tell the churches of his constant intercession for them. He told the Galatians that he would labor (which includes prayer) so that Christ would be formed in them. Teachers travail for the Body by seeking Christ for greater revelation of the scriptures.

My little children, of whom I travail in birth again until Christ be formed in you...Gal 4:19 (KJV)

Conversely, we know that Jesus challenges all believers to be consistent in prayer. In addition, the scriptures continually admonish believers to be intercessors for one another. Again, consistent intercession for others and spiritual truth may be a sign of the call to teach, not the manifestation of it.

We have already established that TEACHERS MUST HAVE A DEFINTE CALL

FROM THE LORD. The above signs are only indications of a call to teach.

Once a call to teach is established, the teacher goes through training and discipline. In the next chapter, we will discuss the making of a teacher. Exercising great knowledge and understanding through the Spirit is not the hallmark of the teacher's ministry; it is his character. Therefore, Christ builds the teacher to reflect His nature.

-Chapter 3-

The Office of the

Teacher

Teaching ministry is important. Though there are differences in the administration and demonstration of teaching gifts, all teachers have essentially the same functions within the Church.

Nine Functions of the Teaching Office

Teach the Word of God. Teachers are endowed by Jesus Christ to teach the scriptures.

They have the God-given ability to interpret the meaning and application of the scriptures. This is the primary function of the teacher; that is, to teach.

Anyone who claims a call to this office and has no clear revelation and understanding of the scriptures may not really be called. It is impossible to claim the teaching office without an ability to teach.

> *So when they had dined, Jesus saith to Simon Peter, Simon, son of Jonas, lovest thou me more than these? He saith unto him, Yea, Lord; thou knowest that I love thee. He saith unto him, Feed my lambs. (John 21:15)*

When Jesus appeared to the disciples

on the shore, He gave Peter one command. Every teacher has this command on their lives: feed the people of God.

Serve as Authors. Because teachers reveal foundational truths of the faith, many of them will write the things that God imparts to them.

The New Testament is comprised of letters that the apostles wrote to teach believers concerning the faith. Though Paul was an apostle, he was also a teacher. His teaching ministry was evident in his letters.

Thus speaketh the Lord God of Israel, saying, Write thee all the words that I have spoken unto thee in a book. (Jeremiah 30:2)

Jeremiah was instructed to write down the prophetic revelation God gave. Some teachers therefore will write the principles and revelations that God gives.

Reaffirm Spiritual Foundations. Teachers have the authority and anointing to reaffirm spiritual foundations in the Church. In the New Testament church, God set teachers in place after the apostles and prophets.

This was so that they could establish people in the foundational truth revealed by the apostles and prophets.

And are built upon the foundation of the apostles and prophets, Jesus Christ himself being the chief corner stone. (Ephesians 2:20)

Paul and Apollos worked together at the Corinthian church. Paul planted through the apostolic ministry and Apollos watered through the teaching ministry within him.

Explain the use and function of Spiritual Gifts (I Timothy 4:14). Teachers have the ability to categorize and explain the use and functions of the gifts of God. They have the ability to teach men how to recognize the gifts within them and when they are in operation.

Teachers sometimes are used to reveal gifts in believers and impart gifts (by the direction of the Spirit) through the laying on of hands. Teachers were involved in launching Paul and Barnabas into the apostolic ministry.

Now there were in the church that was at Antioch certain prophets and teachers; as Barnabas, and Simeon that was called Niger, and Lucius of Cyrene, and Manaen, which had been brought up with Herod the tetrarch, and Saul. As they ministered to the Lord, and fasted, the Holy Ghost said, Separate me Barnabas and Saul for the work whereunto I have called them. And when they had fasted and prayed, and laid their hands on them, they sent them away. (Acts 13:1-3)

Establish Schools and Training Facilities. To provide a structured format for the execution of their ministries, some teachers will establish schools of ministry and training facilities for believers to receive sound doctrine concerning the faith.

Most teachers have a desire to teach and train others how to present the word of God in an effective manner. Thus, like the schools of the prophets in the Old Testament, teachers set us numerous training stations and schools to promote information and revelation of the faith.

Interpret Hard Sayings and Scriptures. Through the revelation of the Spirit, teachers can explain mysteries that are presented in the word of God.

Again, Paul presented the gospel at Corinth. However, Apollos (a skilled teacher) watered the saints by building on Paul's initial ministry through teaching.

> *I have planted, Apollos watered; but God gave the increase. (I Corinthians 3:6)*

Expose False Doctrines. Teachers are excellent apologists of the word of God. They are gifted to expose false doctrines. A true teacher will know how to defend the faith against heresy and expose doctrines that are detrimental to the Church.

Teachers, like the prophets of old, will unashamedly cry out against false doctrines and the ministers that promote them.

> *The prophets prophesy falsely, and the priests bear rule by their means; and my people love to have it so: and what will ye do in the end thereof? (Jeremiah 5:31)*

Perform Signs, Wonders and Healings. Signs and wonders should follow their ministries. Those who are called to this office should expect God to move in their ministries. God always confirms His word.

The teacher's primary ministry is to expound upon the Word. The Word is most effective when it is taught and demonstrated (signs and wonders following).

The same came to Jesus by night, and said unto him, Rabbi, we know that thou art a teacher come from God: for no man can do these miracles that thou doest, except God be with him.(John 3:2)

Jesus, as a teacher, had miracles in His ministry. The New Testament teacher should follow His example. Teachers must be careful not to become so dogmatic that they do not allow the Spirit of God to flow freely.

Establish Believers, Churches, and Organizations in the Faith through Doctrinal Purity. Teachers have the chore to bring the people back to the purity of the faith. They have the ability to promote growth and stability in the Body of Christ.

In addition, through their ministries, they will endeavor to make sure that the word of God is presented with sound wisdom and insight.

Knowledge of the office of the teacher is important to understanding the work of Christ in the Church. Illumination helps to develop an appreciation for these ministries and a desire to see it in operation along with the apostles, prophets, pastors, and evangelists.

Focus of Teachers

Teachers work to see that the believers have the right information that will lead them to God. Teachers are concerned for the growth and stability of the Church.

However, their task is to promote these things through proper explanation and application of the scriptures. They will have insight into what God is saying in the scriptures.

However, they must be careful not to misinterpret God's personal involvement in an individual's life by the misappropriation of scriptures.

-Chapter 4-

The Roles of the Teacher

Teachers will vary in demonstration and execution of their ministries. From numerous examples in scripture, we know that teachers have an important role in the Body of Christ.

Now there are diversities of gifts, but the same Spirit. And there are differences of administrations, but the same Lord. And there are diversities of operations, but it is the same God which worketh all in all. (I Corinthians 12:4-6)

Though not all teachers are the same, there are certain characteristics that they possess. All teachers exhibit characteristics of instructors and trainers.

Teachers as Instructors

God calls teachers for one purpose. They are to be His instructors in the Church. They are given to help people not only understand the mysteries of God, but also provide instruction for practical application of the truths that are presented.

Instructors are experts in their field. An instructor, regardless of subject matter, has a profound understanding of the subject he/she teaches. They are able to present their subject matter because of their personal knowledge.

The teacher is the same. He is able to present the truths of God's word because of the impartation of understanding given by the Holy Spirit.

Which things also we speak, not in the words which man's wisdom teacheth, but which the Holy Ghost teacheth; comparing spiritual things with spiritual. (I Corinthians 2:13)

Instructors provide vital information. Instructors will give information that is important to understanding the subject.

Instructors give information relative to their subject matter. The New Testament teacher functions similarly in the Church.

> *And thou shalt teach them ordinances and laws, and shalt shew them the way wherein they must walk, and the work that they must do. (Exodus 18:20)*

Instructors provide instructions for application of information presented. Good instructors provide information and tools for application. Their students will learn how to apply the information learned in real life environments. Anointed teachers do the same for believers. They know how to present the letter of the Word and minister under the inspiration of the Spirit to edify believers. They will be encouraged to apply what they have learned.

Now therefore hearken, O Israel, unto the statutes and unto the judgments, which I teach you, for to do them, that ye may live... (Deuteronomy 4:1)

Teachers as Trainers

Weight loss is a hot topic today. Many people hire trainers to help them in the efforts to shed unwanted pounds. Teachers function in a similar manner in the Body of Christ.

Trainers are examples of the programs they prescribe. The best trainers are those who have tried their own systems. Trainers who have tested their prescribed programs know how to effectively take others through the process. The New Testament teacher is a demonstrator of the truths that he/she teaches.

> *The husbandman that laboureth must be first partaker of the fruits.*
> *(2 Timothy 2:6)*

The teacher's conduct will exemplify their doctrine and ministry.

Trainers know how to apply their prescribed programs to different individuals. Skilled trainers know how to tailor their systems to fit the person whom they are training. This demonstrates the versatility of the program and of the trainer.

Teachers have to be able to do the same thing as they execute their ministries.

> *And unto the Jews I became as a Jew, that I might gain the Jews; to them that are under the law, as under the*

law, that I migh gain them that are under the law; To them that are without law, as without law, (being not without law to God, but under the law to Christ,) that I might gain them that are without law. To the weak became I as weak, that I might gain the weak: I am made all things to all men, that I might by all means save some. (I Corinthians 9:20-22)

They know how to make the Word of God communicable to different types of people. This is to ensure that all will grow and mature in their knowledge of the

Lord.

Trainers know how to interpret and apply their prescribed programs effectively. Trainers know how to prescribe the requirements of their particular programs.

They know which parts to apply and when to apply them. Teachers are skilled at interpreting and presenting the Word of God. They know how to apply biblical principles to everyday Christian living.

Study to shew thyself approved unto God, a workman that needeth not to be ashamed, rightly dividing the word of truth. (2 Timothy 2:15)

Teaching Disciples

The outpouring of the Spirit gave all believers the ability to understand and explain Him through the Word. The apostles instructed the believers to teach one another in various manners.

We must remember that some believers are gifted by God to teach without occupying the office of the Teacher. These people are referred to as teaching disciples.

For a full examination of the teaching disciple, please see my book, "The Training of the Teaching Disciple: The Preparation of the Teaching Disciple for Ministry and Service."

-Chapter 5-

False Teachers

There is still much to be learned about the teaching ministry and anointing. However, understanding comes with responsibility. God is setting a new standard for all ministers, ministries, and laymen to follow. The Church has to stand against deception. The scriptures are clear that the number of false ministers will increase as the end of this age approaches.

Not every individual preaching in the name of the Lord is His servant. The enemy seeks to destroy the work of God in the earth through imitation. Therefore, the enemy sets his false ministers in the Church to undermine the work of God's chosen vessels.

False ministers are here, but the saints are not to be afraid of falling into deception. False ministers provide a service to the Church. How?

> *For there must be also heresies among*
>
> *you, that they which are approved may be made manifest among you. (I Corinthians 11:19)*

When Paul used the word heresies, he was speaking of divisions and those that caused them. False ministers seek to keep the Church in perpetual dissension and division. Their ministries put enmity between believers with the intent to create a following for themselves.

The answer to "How do false ministers provide a service to the Church?" seems non-existent. However, the statement of Paul provides a simple explanation.

False ministers help us to recognize true ministers of God. Paul said that there must be heresies (and those that cause them) among you so that those who are approved (right, true, anointed, etc.) might be made visible. The ministries of false ministers demonstrate to the Church the improper way to minister. Therefore, when true ministry is in operation, it can be received without fear.

Characteristics of False Ministers

We cannot end our discussion of teachers without talking about false teachers. Before examining false teachers exclusively, it is imperative that we are able to recognize the characteristics of any false minister (or layman). Jesus gave this warning concerning false ministers.

Beware of false prophets, which come to you in sheep's clothing, but inwardly they are ravening wolves. Ye shall know them by their fruits. Do men gather grapes of thorns, or figs of thistles? Even so every good tree bringeth forth good fruit; but a corrupt tree bringeth forth evil fruit. A good tree cannot bring forth evil fruit, neither can a corrupt tree bring forth good fruit. Every tree that bringeth not forth good fruit is hewn down, and cast into the fire.

Wherefore by their fruits ye shall know them. (Matthew 7:15-20)

One true way to recognize false ministers is by the fruit that they bear. Fruit refers to their lifestyles and not their ministries. Moreover, not everyone that is false calls himself an apostle or prophet. Though false apostles and prophets exist, there are also false evangelists, pastors, and teachers. Regardless of the title that a false minister has, he (or she) will exhibit the following characteristics.

They preach that godliness is gain. Godliness to false ministers means prosperity and healing. They seldom teach against sin. They promote serving God for what you can get.

> *If any man teach otherwise, and consent not to wholesome words, even the words of our Lord Jesus Christ, and to the doctrine which is according to godliness; He is proud, knowing nothing, but doting about questions and strifes of words, whereof cometh envy, strife, railings, evil surmisings, perverse disputings of men of corrupt minds, and destitute of the truth, supposing that*

gain is godliness: from such withdraw thyself. (I Timothy 6:3-5)

They only teach that you belong to God and should have the best. They promote the concept that God only wants you blessed, without declaring that God also wants character, integrity, and holiness in His people.

Their doctrine focuses on the miraculous work of God and His blessings, exclusively. They promote God's blessing, rather than God and His Christ. They teach individuals how to prosper in God without living for Him.

They were once servants of God. Many false ministers have genuine conversion experiences. They entered ministry by the call of God. However, consistent rebellion, sin, pride, and greed caused them to error from the truth.

For if after they have escaped the pollutions of the world through the knowledge of the Lord and Saviour Jesus Christ, they are again entangled therein, and overcome, the latter end is worse with them than the beginning. For it had been better for them not to have known the way of righteousness, than, after they have known it, to turn from the holy commandment delivered unto them. But it is happened unto them according to the true proverb, the dog is turned to his own vomit again; and the sow that was washed to her wallowing in the mire. (II Peter 2:20-22)

Peter wrote that false ministers did escape the pollutions of the world by Christ. However, they returned to their sins and filthy ways. Consequently, Peter added, they are worse than they were before their initial conversion. It serves as a warning to every minister. If the love of money, pride, and sin are not rejected, the road to becoming an enemy of God becomes inevitable.

Characteristics of False Teachers

False teachers will demonstrate the same behavior as other false ministers. However, there will be certain traits that are readily visible in false teaching ministers.

They operate in false authority. False teachers do not operate in godly authority. They establish their own authority in the Body of Christ. They disguise their wickedness by first appearing as true servants of Christ.

> *For such are false apostles, deceitful workers, transforming themselves into the apostles of Christ. And no marvel; for Satan himself is transformed into an angel of light. Therefore it is no great thing if his ministers also be transformed as the ministers of righteousness; whose end shall be according to their works. (II Corinthians 11:13-15)*

Paul stated that those who are false would resemble those who are true. However, once they have gained some respect, they will attack other leaders. The false apostles and leaders of Paul's day tried to defame him and establish their own authority in the churches. False teachers use this tactic today. Through the defamation of others, they exalt their personal ministries.

Another tactic used is misinterpretation of scripture to establish authority. They find scriptures that refer to ministerial authority and claim it for themselves. They promote themselves to the offices of the apostle or prophet to give credence to their ministries. They try to walk in the calling of others, which turns into manipulation and deception.

True teachers will be humble men and women with a servant's heart. They will not promote their personal ministries. The authority that they operate in is backed by the power of God and is recognized in the Church.

They operate in counterfeit gifts. False teachers minister with the wrong motives. Therefore, the Spirit of God withdraws

Himself from their ministries. Since false teachers want to appear spiritual, they strive to operate in 'gifts' to validate the ministry. They begin to rely on their own human spirit and help from demonic influence to appear spiritual. This happened to King Saul.

> *But the Spirit of the Lord departed from Saul, and an evil spirit from the Lord troubled him. (I Samuel 16:14)*
>
> *And it came to pass on the morrow, that the evil spirit from God came upon Saul, and he prophesied in the midst of the house: and David*

played with his hand, as at other times: and there was a javelin in Saul's hand. (I Samuel 18:10)

Because of Saul's continual rebellion, the Spirit of God departed from him. An evil spirit replaced God's Spirit. When the evil spirit came upon him, he prophesied. His prophecy came from the wrong source. This eventually happens to false teachers. The Holy Spirit lifts and they use demonic influence to still function.

They twist the scriptures. Another tactic used is misinterpretation of scripture to establish authority. They find scriptures that refer to ministerial authority and claim it for themselves. They scare believers into thinking that because they are ministers, they are superior to others.

They possess a controlling spirit. False teachers will use manipulation to gain followers. Once people begin to follow them, they scare the individuals into staying and/or following them. They tell individuals that if they discontinue fellowship with them or their ministries, God will not be pleased and the like.

In addition, false teacher will try to control

the people's personal lives through biblical misinterpretation. By using false authority, they will tell people who they can marry and where to work. False teachers operate in a similar fashion to cult leaders.

Though false pastors, teachers, and ministers exist, believers are not to walk in fear. However, Christians have to be able to learn to recognize false ministers.

In addition, the presence of false ministers should give believers a greater appreciation for godly leaders and ministries within the Church.

THE BELIEVER'S GUIDE TO THE TEACHING MINISTRY A Comprehensive Study of the Teaching Ministry in the Church

-Book 3-

The Training of the Teaching Disciple:

The Preparation of the Teaching Disciple for Ministry and Service

Introduction

Ministry and service in the kingdom of God is a privilege. God calls every member of the Body of Christ to serve for the benefit and welfare of the Body of Christ. However, we must remember that there are personal preparations that God requires for service.

The Potter's Wheel Study Series is designed to help believers recognize and apply the personal preparation that God implements for those called to minister and to serve.

It is our prayer that the minister and the laymen will respond to God's personal preparations for ministry and service.

In this Publication

Though God uses teachers, they are not the only individuals who are able to teach the scriptures. One of the promises of the New Covenant was that all would be able to understand the law and counsel of God. It would be written on the hearts of His followers.

For this is the covenant that I will make with the house of Israel after those days, saith the Lord; I will put my laws into their mind, and write them in their hearts: and I will be to them a God, and they shall be to me a people. (Hebrews 8:10)

In this book, we will examine those who have a teaching anointing and gift. The outpouring of the Spirit gave all believers the ability to understand and explain Him through the Word. The apostles instructed the believers to teach one another in various manners.

Let the word of Christ dwell in you richly in all wisdom; teaching and admonishing one another in psalms and hymns and spiritual songs, singing with grace in your hearts to the Lord. (Colossians 3:16)

We must remember that some believers are gifted by God to teach without occupying the office of the

Teacher. These people are referred to as teaching disciples. God has a preparation process for those who will operate in the teaching anointing and grace. Learn to accept God's method for successful service.

THE BELIEVER'S GUIDE TO THE TEACHING MINISTRY

A Comprehensive Study of the Teaching Ministry in the Church

-Prologue-
Understanding Anointings

Today, believers worldwide have developed an appreciation for spiritual gifts and manifestations. However, misinterpretations of scripture have caused individuals to boast in possessing "anointings" that do not exist.

Before exploring the teaching anointing, we must develop a clear understanding of the anointing. Both the Old and New Testaments contain numerous references to the anointing.

The anointing is an important component in the service of the Lord. Under both covenants, the servants of the Lord could not serve without it.

The Hebrew and Greek terms for "to anoint" denote to smear or rub in. This implies that the anointing becomes a part of the individual who has received it.

Anointings in the Old Testament

The scriptures tell us that there are diversities of anointings. This was true even under the Old Covenant.

The Hebrew term for anointing was mashchah (pronounced mash-khaw'). It means a consecratory gift and also to consecrate. This implies that the anointed individuals were gifts to those they ministered to. In addition, they were set aside unto the purpose for which they were anointed.

In the Old Testaments texts, God anointed individuals to perform various tasks and stand in certain offices. They were anointed to stand in the offices of priest and king, through oil being poured upon them.

Aaron anointed as a priest

And thou shalt put them upon Aaron thy brother, and his sons with him; and shalt anoint them, and

> *consecrate them, and sanctify them, that they may minister unto me in the priest's office. (Exodus 28: 41)*

David anointed king by Samuel

> *Then Samuel took the horn of oil, and anointed him in the midst of his brethren: and the Spirit of the Lord came upon David (I Samuel 16:13a)*

In each of these examples, the anointing of God was demonstrated by a physical anointing of the individual. However, others were anointed to stand in positions of authority without an outward anointing.

The Judges

> *Nevertheless the Lord raised up judges, which delivered them out of the hand of those that spoiled them. (Judges 2:16)*

The Prophets

> *Since the day that your fathers came forth out of the land of Egypt unto this day I have even sent unto you all my servants the prophets, daily rising up early and sending them. (Jeremiah 7:25)*

It is clear that God raised up the judges and prophets to stand in positions of great authority without an anointing ceremony. The Spirit of God anointed them. We discover that no one could function in any of the above offices except God placed them.

Though there were other individuals whom the Lord used, we find that God anointed individuals to stand as prophets, judges, priests, and kings continually.

In addition, there were other individuals anointed by God to function in other capacities without an anointing ceremony. Individuals such as the builders of the tabernacle, the seventy elders who prophesied after receiving Moses' spirit, Barak, Ezra, Nehemiah, Zerubbabel, and various others. They received an anointing from God to accomplish specific tasks.

Anointings in the New Testament

After Christ's resurrection and the outpouring of the Spirit, we find that God still anointed individuals for service.

We discover from the scriptures that men and women are anointed to stand in ministry offices such as apostles, prophets, evangelists, pastors, and teachers.

And he gave some, apostles; and some, prophets; and some, evangelists; and some, pastors and teachers. (Ephesians 4:11)

Likewise, aside from functioning in ministry offices, individuals are anointed and endowed with certain gifts for Christian service. These other gifts and offices are listed in the book of I Corinthians and in the Book of Romans.

But the manifestation of the Spirit is given to every man to profit withal. For to one is given by the Spirit the word of wisdom; to another the word of knowledge by the same Spirit; To another faith by the same Spirit; to another the gifts of healing by the same Spirit; To another the working of miracles; to another prophecy; to another discerning of spirits; to another divers kinds of tongues; to another the interpretation of tongues. (I Corinthians 12:7-10)

Having then gifts differing according to the grace that is given to us, whether prophecy, let us prophesy according to the proportion of faith;

Or ministry, let us wait on our ministering: or he that teacheth, on teaching; Or he that exhorteth, on exhortation: he that giveth, let him do it with simplicity; he that ruleth, with diligence; he that sheweth mercy, with cheerfulness. (Romans 12:6-8)

Though various terms are used in the New Testament to describe the anointing of the Spirit, two terms are seen frequently. The first is found in II Corinthians 2:21,

Now he which stablisheth us with

you in Christ, and hath anointed us, is God. (2 Corinthians 1:21 KJV)

The Greek work for anointed in this text is chrio (pronounced khree'-o). It means to be consecrated to an office or religious service. Paul used this term to express that God had placed him in the apostolic office to minister to the Church.

Thus, we find that one receives an anointing to serve. If you are not called to a ministry office, there is an anointing on you to serve in some capacity. The second term used for anointing is found in I John 2:20,

But the anointing which ye have received of him abideth in you, and ye need not that any man teach you: but as the same anointing teacheth you of all things, and is truth, and is no lie, and even as it hath taught you, ye shall abide in him. (I John 2:27 KJV)

The Greek word used here is chrisma (pronounced khris'- mah). We derive the word charisma from this word. It is defined as the special endowment of the Holy Spirit. Hence, the anointing comes with gifts and endowments from God.

Therefore, as believers, we should consider the use of the expression, "I am anointed to do such and such" carefully. We must not confuse personal gifts and talents with the endowment of the Spirit.

When we receive the Spirit of God, its presence abides in us. The same is true for the anointing. When God places a particular anointing upon an individual, it remains. The gifts of God will operate according to the need and purpose of the moment.

However, the "anointings" or endowments of the Spirit abide with an individual at all times. Even in disobedience, the anointing to be king remained upon Saul. David recognized this (I Samuel 24:6).

Office versus Anointing

The Spirit of God governs all of the spiritual activities within the Body. He anoints and appoints according to the ultimate will of the Father.

Since the Body of Christ is made up of many members, there are various needs within it. The Spirit of God then anoints individuals to fulfill the needs within the Body.

The greatest burden for ministry rests upon the leaders, specifically, the apostles, prophets, evangelists, pastors, and teachers. Their purpose is found in Ephesians 4:12:

1. 1.To perfect the saints
2. To train them for the work of the ministry
3. To build up the Church spiritually

However, these ministries are not responsible to minister to everyone. God uses the entire Body of Christ. The members of the Body of Christ are called to minister to one another, even if they are not called to a ministry office.

As every man hath received the gift, even so minister the same one toward another, as good stewards over the manifold grace of God. (I Peter 4:10)

Therefore, God anoints individuals to function in similar ways to those of the ministry offices.

Believers will have anointings on their lives, which, if not careful, may be mistaken for a call to a particular ministry office. This implies that there are some that have an apostolic gift without being called as an apostle.

Moreover, some have an anointing to prophesy without functioning in the office of the prophet. This is also true for teachers.

Numerous individuals today have laid claim to a teaching anointing without understanding all that they entail. Remember to never confuse a call to a ministry office with an anointing of the Holy Spirit. However, an individual with a teaching anointing is identified as a teaching disciple.

With this brief analysis of the anointing, we will now explore the teaching anointing and how God prepares one for this gift and ministry in the Church.

-Chapter 1-

Teaching Disciples as Instructors

Teaching disciples are called for one purpose. They are in the Body of Christ to ensure that valid teaching and doctrine is promoted in the Body of Christ. Teaching disciples have the same responsibilities of the Teacher. However, the scope and authority of their gifting is less than that of the Teacher.

Skilled in Function

Instructors are experts in their field. An instructor, regardless of subject matter, has a profound understanding of the subject he/she teaches. They are able to present their subject matter because of their personal knowledge.

The teaching disciple is the same. He is able to present the truths of God's word because of the impartation of understanding given by the Holy Spirit.

Which things also we speak, not in the words which man's wisdom teacheth, but which the Holy Ghost teacheth; comparing spiritual things with spiritual. (I Corinthians 2:13)

Skilled in Information

Instructors provide vital information. Instructors will give information that is important to understanding the subject.

Instructors give information relative to their subject matter. The teaching disciple functions similarly in the Church.

And thou shalt teach them ordinances and laws, and shalt shew them the way wherein they must walk, and the work that they must do. (Exodus 18:20)

Skilled in Instruction

Instructors provide instructions for application of information presented. Good instructors provide information and tools for application. Their students will learn how to apply the information learned in real life environments.

Teaching disciples do the same for other believers. They know how to present the letter of the Word and minister under the inspiration of the Spirit to edify believers. They will be encouraged to apply what they have learned.

> *Now therefore hearken, O Israel, unto the statutes and unto the judgments, which I teach you, for to do them, that ye may live... (Deuteronomy 4:1)*

THE BELIEVER'S GUIDE TO THE TEACHING MINISTRY

A Comprehensive Study of the Teaching Ministry in the Church

-Chapter 2-

Teaching Disciples as Tutors

To aid in a student's education, tutors are employed to reinforce and explain what is taught in the classroom. Teaching disciples provide extra support, strength, and encouragement to other members.

Teach from Experience

Tutors teach the things that they have learned. The best tutors are those who tutor others in subjects that they have mastered.

Tutors know the 'ends' and 'outs' of their subjects and know how to effectively communicate it to others. The teaching disciple is a demonstrator of the truths that he/she teaches.

The husbandman that laboureth must be first partaker of the fruits. (2 Timothy 2:6)

The teaching disciple's conduct will exemplify their doctrine.

Teach from Versatility

Tutors know how to present their subjects to different individuals. Effective tutors know how to tailor their instruction to fit the person whom they are tutoring. This demonstrates the versatility of the tutor. Teaching disciples have to be able to do the same thing as they minister to others in the Church.

And unto the Jews I became as a Jew, that I might gain the Jews; to them that are under the law, as under the law, that I might gain them that are under the law; To them that are without law, as without law, (being not without law to God, but under the law to Christ,) that I might gain them that are without law. To the weak became I as weak, that I might gain the weak: I am made all things to all men, that I might by all means save some. (I Corinthians 9:20-22)

They know how to make the Word of God communicable to different types of people. This is to ensure that all will grow and mature in their knowledge of the Lord.

Teach through Application

Tutors know how to interpret different aspects of their subjects and communicate them to their tutees. Tutors know how to tailor their lessons to fit their students.

They know which parts to apply and how to apply them. teaching disciples are skilled at interpreting and presenting the Word of God. They know how to apply biblical principles to everyday Christian living.

Study to shew thyself approved unto God, a that needeth not to be ashamed, rightly dividing the word of truth. (2 Timothy 2:15)

-Chapter 3-

Character Traits of Teaching Disciples

Because teaching people have a God-given understanding of spiritual truths through the Word, their characters have to be developed and be conducive to the teaching ministry.

Without character, teaching disciples will become deceived, prideful, and move in a realm that is reserved only for those who are called as teachers. Jesus' "Sermon on the Mount" began with what is called "The Beatitudes" (Matthew 5:3-12).

Teaching people must use Jesus' words to govern their characters. These same traits are required for those possessing a teaching anointing.

Humility of the Teaching Disciple

Blessed are the poor in spirit. Teaching Disciples have to be humble. Because God uses them to communicate His messages, humility will bring stability to them and protect them against deception.

Blessed are those who mourn. Teaching disciples have to be broken before God. They should grieve over the sins of the Church and make intercession to God on behalf of the people.

Blessed are those who are meek. Teaching Disciples have to be mild-mannered and even-tempered.

They cannot be governed by their their emotions, nor bound by biases and anger. Though God may use them to challenge others, they have to do it in the proper spirit.

Hallmarks of the Teaching Disciple

Blessed are those who hunger and thirst for righteousness. Teaching Disciples have to be holy. Their daily task is to reflect the holiness and of God in their walk with Him.

Blessed are those who are merciful. Teaching disciples should be compassionate and forgiving. Compassion will help them to minister without condemnation, while forgiveness will keep their hearts pure toward others eve in light of persecution, rejection, and misunderstanding.

Blessed are the pure in heart. Teaching disciples must have the right motives in ministering. They do not minister for popularity or position, but because of the love of God and the brethren. Again, if these do not govern teaching disciples, they leave themselves open for a snare and trap of the devil.

-Chapter 4-

Identifying the Teaching Anointing

Teaching disciples are dispersed in the Body by the discretion of the Spirit. Some people who possess a teaching anointing do not recognize it.

To aid in the identification of the teaching anointing, let us look at how teaching disciples will function within the Body.

Teachers of the Word

Teaching disciples teach the Word of God. Teaching know how to interpret soundly the scriptures. They boldly teach the Word. The written Word must live in them before they can teach others.

Let the word of Christ dwell in you richly in all wisdom; teaching and admonishing one another in psalms and hymns and spiritual songs, singing with grace in your hearts to the Lord. (Colossians 3:16)

Teachers of Application

Teaching disciples are tutors. Teaching disciples have the ability to explain truths to others. They are able to break down truth presented by leadership so that others can learn and grow.

They take the burdens of others upon themselves and show them how to overcome through the Word.

Let every one of us please his neighbour for his good to edification. For even Christ pleased not himself; but, as it is written, The reproaches of them that reproached thee fell on me. (Romans 15:2-3)

Teachers of Action

Teaching disciples motivate believers to study the word of God. Teaching Disciples have the ability to motivate others to want to study the word of God. Through the knowledge and presentation of the scriptures, they stir up others to want to know more of the Word.

Teaching disciples declare the prophetic word of the Lord. Many teaching disciples have the gift of prophecy. However, their prophetic words will not have the same anointing, clarity, and depth of someone with a prophetic anointing and ministry. The gift of prophecy brings balance to the teaching gift within them.

But he that prophesieth speaketh unto men to edification, and exhortation, and comfort. He that speaketh in an unknown tongue edifieth himself; but he that prophesieth edifieth the church. (I Corinthians 14:3)

Teachers of Interpretation

Teaching disciples interpret difficult passages of scripture. Through the revelation of the Spirit, teaching disciples can explain mysteries that are presented in the word of God. They are able to bring clarity to biblical truths that may seem unclear or controversial.

In addition to interpreting scriptures, teaching disciples will expose false ministers and doctrines. Teaching Disciples have the spiritual insight to recognize error. Through the revelation of the Spirit and by their knowledge of the Word, they warn others against deception and false ministry.

> *Beloved, believe not every spirit, but try the spirits whether they are of God: because many false prophets are gone out into the world. (I John 4:1)*

Teaching disciples have other gifts operating in them. Along with the teaching gift, teaching disciples have other gifts of the Spirit. Most common among them is the discerning of spirits, the word of knowledge, and the word of wisdom.

But all these worketh that one and the selfsame Spirit, dividing to every man severally as he will. (I Corinthians 12:11)

-Chapter 5-

Walking in the Teaching Anointing

If you feel you have a teaching anointing upon your life, it will not flourish if you are not consistent in your relationship with the Lord. The following steps are necessary to walk consistently in a teaching anointing.

Consistent Study

Teaching disciples have to consistently study and apply the Word of God to their lives. They must remember that every doctrine taught must be in line with the scriptures. If there is no knowledge of the Word, they will teach in error. The written Word is needed for a vibrant ministry.

> *We have also a more sure word of prophecy; whereunto ye do well that ye take heed, as unto a light that shineth in a dark place, until the day dawn, and the daystar arise in your hearts. (II Peter 1:19)*

Persistent Prayer

Teaching disciples have to be consistent in prayer. It is the only way to remain strong in the Lord. Prayer is the vehicle through which revelation of the Word is received. Praying keeps the teaching anointing fresh. If you want to walk in the teaching anointing, an established prayer life is mandatory.

Rejoice evermore. Pray without ceasing. In everything give thanks thanks: for this is the will of God in Christ Jesus concerning you. (I Thessalonians 5:16-18)

Insistent Submission

Teaching disciples have to be submitted to local leadership. They must follow the vision of the leaders as they follow Christ. Though they have a great understanding of the Word, they are not to think they are more spiritual than leadership and other members.

In order for the teaching ministry to remain strong in them, they have to respect the authority that God has placed over them. They have to respect authority before God entrusts them with the authority to teach His word.

For I am a man under authority... (Matthew 8:9a)

The centurion received a blessing from

Christ because he respected His authority. Likewise, teaching disciples will receive revelation of the Word as they respect God-given leadership.

Bibliography

Evans, Roderick L. Now Concerning Teachers: Establishing the Role of the Teacher in the Body of Christ. Abundant Truth Publishing. Camden, NC, 2009

Lockman Foundation. *Comparative Study Bible.* Zondervan Publishing House. Grand Rapids, MI, c1984

Merriam-Webster Online Dictionary

Copyright © 2005 by Merriam-

Webster, Incorporated. All rights reserved.

The Bible Library. *The Bible Library CD Rom Disc.* Ellis Enterprises Incorporated, (c) 1988 – 2000. 4205 McAuley Blvd., Suite 385, Oklahoma City, OK 73120. All Rights Reserved.

www.ingramcontent.com/pod-product-compliance
Lightning Source LLC
Chambersburg PA
CBHW050339010526
44119CB00049B/614